BLOODSUCKERS

OF THE ANIMAL WORLD

by Jody Sullivan Rake

Content Consultant:
David Stephens, PhD
Professor of Ecology, Evolution, and Behavior

Reading Consultant:
Professor Barbara J. Fox

raintree
a Capstone company — publishers for children

Raintree is an imprint of Capstone Global Library Limited, a company incorporated in England and Wales having its registered office at
7 Pilgrim Street, London, EC4V 6LB – Registered company number: 6695582
www.raintree.co.uk
myorders@raintree.co.uk

ISBN 978-1-4062-9173-5
18 17 16 15 14
10 9 8 7 6 5 4 3 2 1

British Library Cataloguing in Publication Data
A full catalogue record for this book is available from the British Library.

Editorial Credits
Abby Colich, editor; Kyle Grenz, designer; Jo Miller, media researcher;
Katy LaVigne, production specialist

Photo Credits
Clinton Bauder, 28-29; Dreamstime: Deyangeorgiev, cover (skin), Joao Estevao Andreade De Freitas, 6-7; Getty Images: De Agostini/Archivio B, 20-21, Oxford Scientific/Roger Eritja, 22-23; Minden Pictures: Jim Clare, 10-11; Newscom: Danita Delimont Photography/Pete Oxford, 12-13, Minden Pictures/Stephen Dalton, 9, Photoshot/NHPA/Agence Nature, 15, Photoshot/NHPA/Image Quest 3-D, 24, Photoshot/NHPA/Roger Tidman, 16-17; Photoshot: NHPA/Paulo de Oliveira, 14; Shutterstock: Henrik Larsson, 25, Kokhanchikov, 4-5, LauraD, 29 (inset), smuay, 18-19; SuperStock: Biosphoto, 26-27, Minden Pictures, cover (bugs)

Printed in China by Nordica.
1014/CA21401515

CONTENTS

REAL VAMPIRES

All animals must eat to survive. Some animal **diets** are unusual. Others are disgusting! Blood is a part of many animal diets.

diet what an animal eats

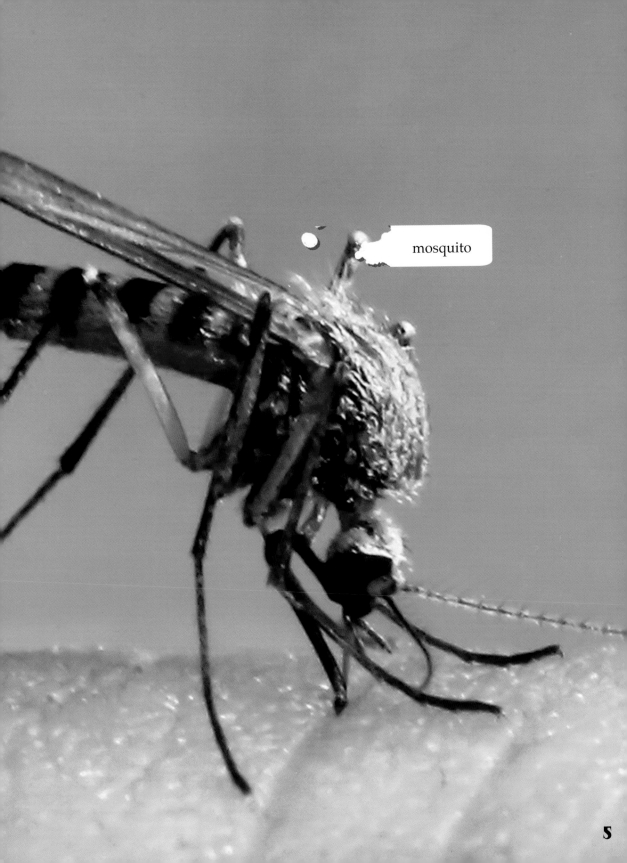

mosquito

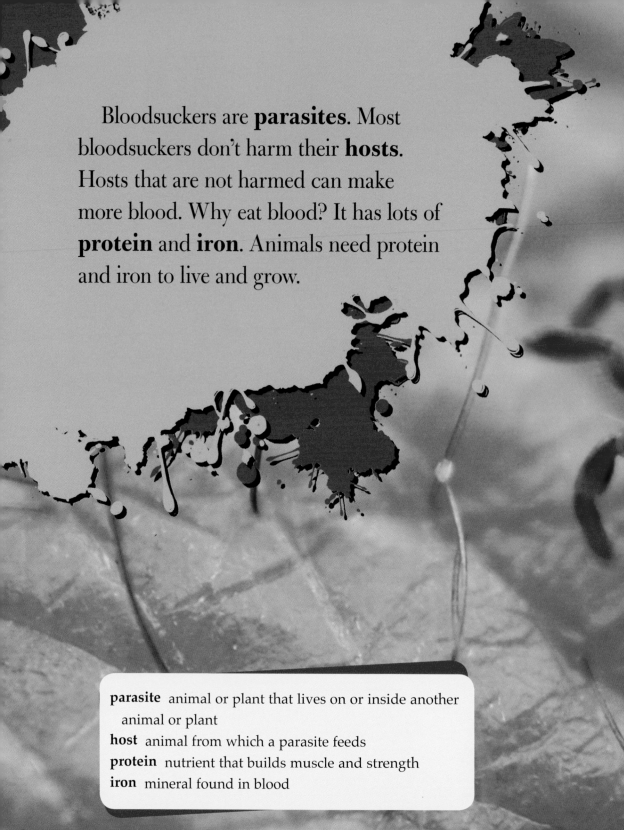

Bloodsuckers are **parasites**. Most bloodsuckers don't harm their **hosts**. Hosts that are not harmed can make more blood. Why eat blood? It has lots of **protein** and **iron**. Animals need protein and iron to live and grow.

parasite animal or plant that lives on or inside another animal or plant
host animal from which a parasite feeds
protein nutrient that builds muscle and strength
iron mineral found in blood

Fact!

Many bloodsuckers have special spit. The spit helps keep the host's blood flowing. This means more food for the bloodsucker.

tick

I WANT TO BITE YOUR ANKLE!

Vampire bats live in Mexico and Central and South America. They earn their name! These bats sleep all day. Then they come out at night to hunt. Vampire bats are the only **mammals** that eat only blood.

Fact!

The common vampire bat sucks blood from cows, pigs and horses. The hairy-legged and white-winged vampire bats eat bird blood.

mammal animal with hair or fur that gives birth to young and feeds them milk

Vampire bats don't usually bite necks. The common vampire bat finds food during flight. It lands near a sleeping animal. Then it crawls close enough to make a small bite in the ankle and licks up the blood.

BLOODTHIRSTY BIRD

Finches are songbirds that eat seeds. When
seeds are scarce, a vampire finch eats blood.
It climbs on to the back of a bird
called a booby and pecks at
the booby's neck. Then the
finch sucks blood from
the tiny wound.

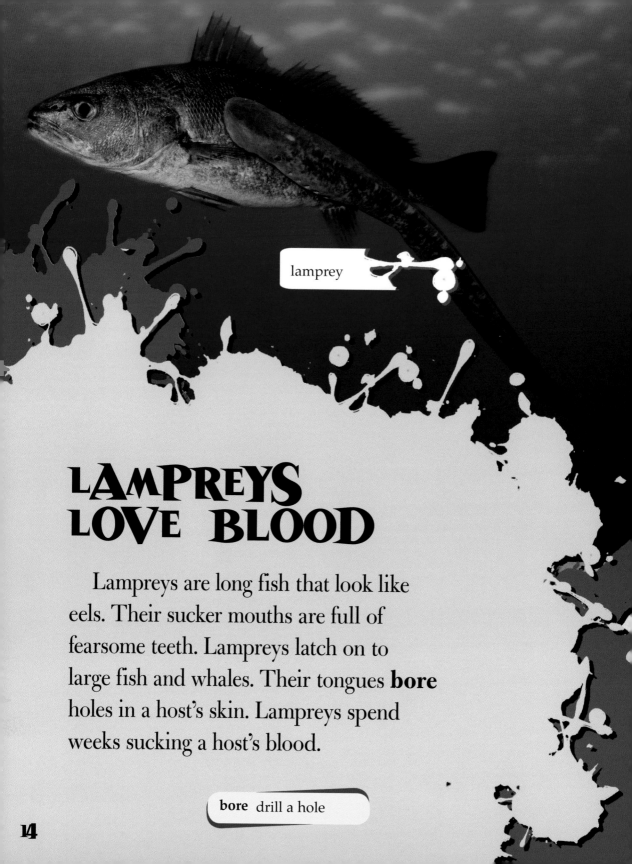

lamprey

LAMPREYS LOVE BLOOD

Lampreys are long fish that look like eels. Their sucker mouths are full of fearsome teeth. Lampreys latch on to large fish and whales. Their tongues **bore** holes in a host's skin. Lampreys spend weeks sucking a host's blood.

bore drill a hole

Fact!

Lampreys are one of the few
bloodsuckers that can kill their hosts.
Many hang on until their victims die.

THE CREEPY CANDIRU

The tiny candiru fish is the size of a toothpick. This little bloodsucker swims into the gills of a larger fish. The candiru finds a **blood vessel** inside its host. Then it settles down for a nice long suck.

blood vessel thin tube that carries blood through the body

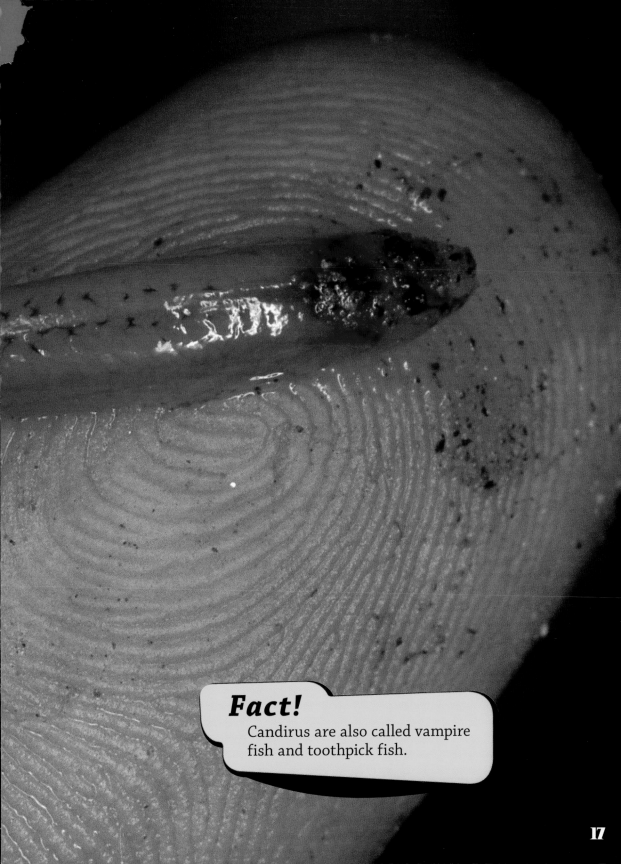

Fact!

Candirus are also called vampire fish and toothpick fish.

THE BUZZ ON MOSQUITOES

Have you ever been bitten by a mosquito? A mosquito leaves spit in your skin. That's what makes the itchy red bump. Only female mosquitoes eat blood. They need it for their eggs.

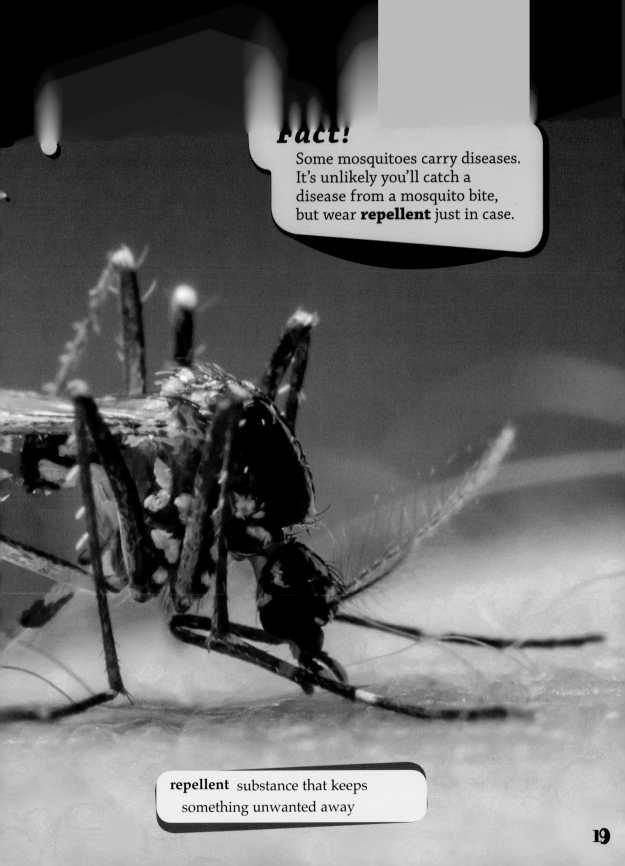

Fact!

Some mosquitoes carry diseases. It's unlikely you'll catch a disease from a mosquito bite, but wear **repellent** just in case.

repellent substance that keeps something unwanted away

PARASITE MOTH

Most moths are harmless **nectar** eaters. The male vampire moth of Siberia is different. Blood is the favourite food of this moth. It uses an extra-long, sharp tongue for poking animal skin and gulping blood!

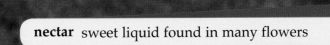

nectar sweet liquid found in many flowers

GOOD NIGHT! SLEEP TIGHT!

A bed bug looks like an apple pip. It hides in furniture, carpet and even books. This bloodsucker sleeps during the day. It comes out at night to bite and suck its host's blood.

Fact!

You won't feel a bed bug bite. Its spit will **numb** your skin before it bites.

numb take away feeling

BUGGED BY BUGS

Many bugs are bloodsuckers.
Fleas feast on the blood of animals
such as dogs and cats. Ticks dine
on the blood of deer and other animals.
They bite humans, too. Be careful!
Like mosquitoes, some ticks spread diseases.

flea

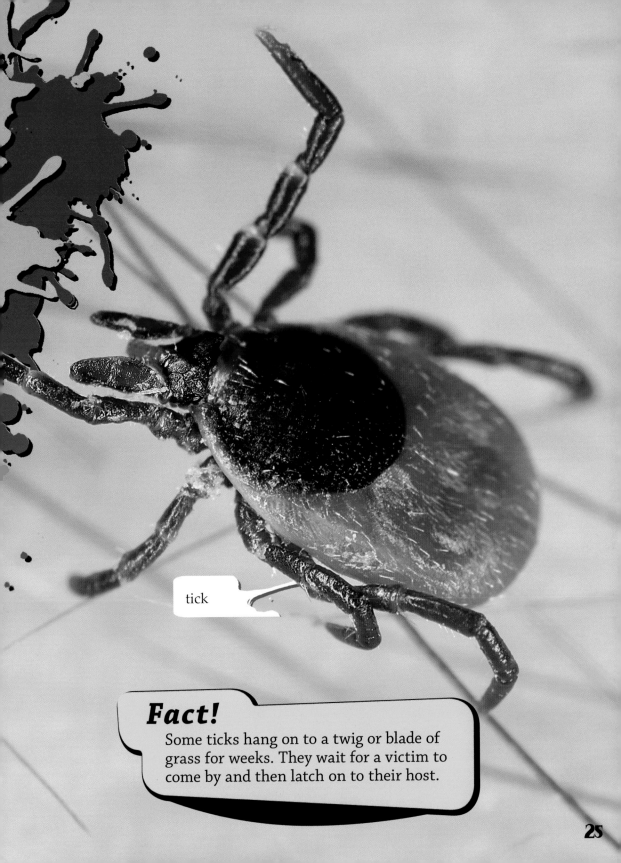

tick

Fact!

Some ticks hang on to a twig or blade of grass for weeks. They wait for a victim to come by and then latch on to their host.

DISGUSTING BUT HELPFUL

Leeches are related to earthworms. Leeches live in lakes, rivers and ponds. A leech has a suction cup on each end of its body. Both ends hold on while one end does the sucking.

Fact!

Doctors have used leeches for thousands of years. Today doctors use leeches to increase blood flow in some patients. Leeches help to heal damaged areas of the human body.

A FuSSY BLOODSuCKING SNAIL

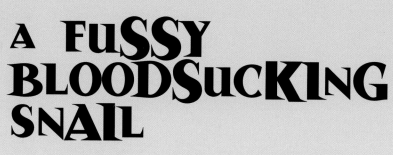

The Cooper's nutmeg snail eats the blood of only one animal – the electric ray. The snail can smell the ray from 23 metres (75 feet) away. It sticks its long, bloodsucking tongue into the underside of the ray.

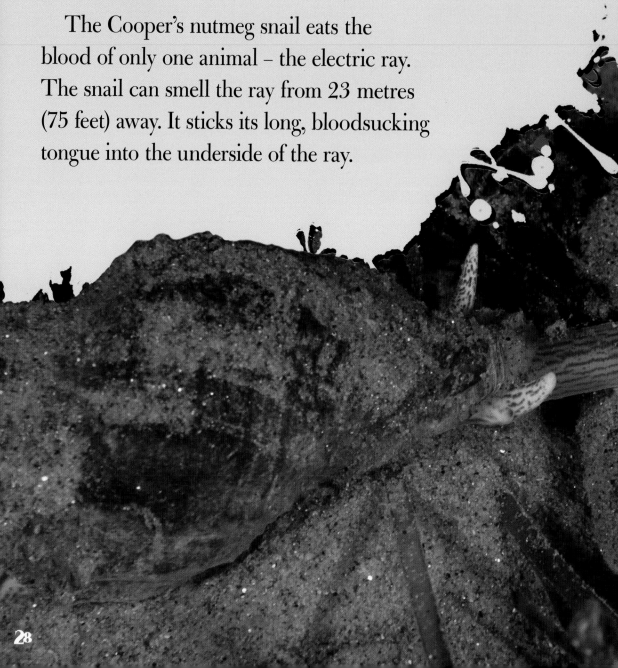

electric ray

Fact!

If there are no electric rays around, the Cooper's nutmeg snail stays buried in the ocean floor. It can go up to 12 days without eating.

GLOSSARY

blood vessel thin tube that carries blood through the body

bore drill a hole

diet what an animal eats

host animal from which a parasite feeds

iron mineral found in blood

mammal animal with hair or fur that gives birth to young and feeds them milk

nectar sweet liquid found in many flowers

numb take away feeling

parasite animal or plant that lives on or inside another animal or plant

protein nutrient that builds muscle and strength

repellent substance that keeps something unwanted away

READ MORE

Bats (Animal Abilities), Charlotte Guillain (Raintree, 2014)

Bloodsucking Lice and Fleas (Creepy Crawlies), Ellen Rodger (Crabtree Publishing, 2010)

In This Bedroom (What's Lurking in this House), Nancy Harris (Raintree, 2010)

WEBSITES

www.bbc.co.uk/nature/life/Common_Vampire_Bat
Find out more about these furry little bloodsuckers, and watch them at work.

www.bbc.co.uk/nature/life/Cephalaspidomorphi
Latest news and information on these bloodsucking sea creatures.

kids.nationalgeographic.com/content/kids/en_US/animals/vampire-bat/
Interesting facts and photos. Learn more about the vampire bat.

INDEX